A HOPEFUL WORLD

conversations with a five year old

HOPE CAMPBELL
EDITED BY: ALLORA CAMPBELL

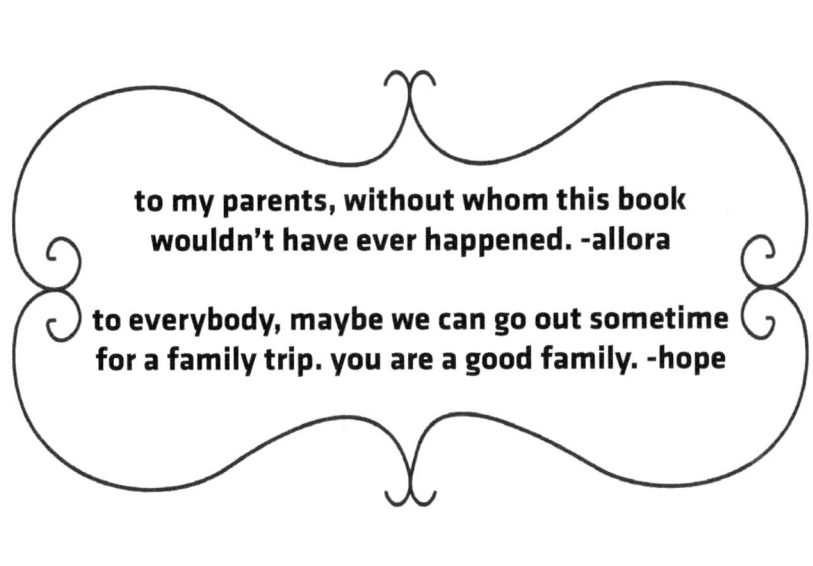

to my parents, without whom this book wouldn't have ever happened. -allora

to everybody, maybe we can go out sometime for a family trip. you are a good family. -hope

TABLE OF CONTENTS

Introduction i

Rules 1

Fashion 10

Homeschool 14

Politics 22

Holidays 27

Technicalities 30

Life 37

Imagination 43

The Natural World 53

Work 64

Faith 70

Family 79

Accomplishments 88

Love 92

Film 96

Discussion 111

INTRODUCTION

I was sixteen--the oldest of nine kids--when Hope, my youngest sister, was born. She was called Hope for two reasons. The first: her birth was supposed to be impossible. A few years before, Mom was diagnosed with a medical ailment that required surgery. The treatment was, consequently, supposed to make any future pregnancies highly improbable. My parents didn't even tell us Mom was pregnant until she was several months along because they had assumed, as had all the doctors, that Hope was not a viable pregnancy.

Second: despite our extensive numbers, we were still a rather new family. My parents had adopted four of my siblings--three, in fact, just two years prior. We were all doing our best to merge together, but the development of our family was still slightly tentative. No matter what, no one could deny the gap in our lives before we had been altogether. We could make new memories together, but there would always be that chunk of time from before we were together. It was different for Hope; she was born into a family that she has never known any other way. Each of her siblings have always been just that. She didn't meet anyone as an adopted or biological sibling. Each of us were as much her brother or sister as the last. You could say (or, at least, we do) that Hope was exactly what we needed.

You can imagine, as the youngest of ten, that she's been spoiled every moment of her existence. We bought her presents, brought home candy from work, volunteered to take her to the store, movies, sleepovers, library visits, parks. Despite all of our very large age gaps (even the second youngest of us is eight years older than her), we all wanted to be around Hope. There is something unique about having a relationship to a sibling so much younger than you. You're technically on the same level--equals--but you're also not. I was starting college, for instance, when Hope was learning to walk. I think there is something of an independence that has rubbed off on her as a result.

We've always bragged that Hope's smart--advanced for her age. But I think there's more to it than that. Maybe I'm just biased, but being around so many older siblings seems to have inspired her.

Just before Hope turned five, I began collecting our conversations and posting them on Facebook. What struck me immediately about the popularity of these posts was that, apparently, I wasn't the only one who loved hearing what Hope had to say. Despite the fact that anything my little sister says is usually more charming and adorable than annoying, there is something bright about our conversations. It's not just innocence—although that is a nearly strong enough descriptor—it's more like being untarnished. My sister is a clean slate, and I always found it refreshing to view the world through her eyes.

The book you now hold is a collection of those sayings, just over a hundred of them, from her year as a five year old. These represent only a fraction of the creativity that bubbles from Hope's mouth on a daily basis, but each and every one always makes me smile. I hope they bring that same joy to your life, because, at least for me, I am very much in need of a hopeful world.

9/27/13

Allora Campbell

CAST

parents:

Dad
Mom

siblings (in age order):

Me (Allora)
Kristen
Amanda
Vanessa
Nicko
Ashley
Anna
Abigail
Justin
Hope

family:

Eppie May (Amanda's daughter)
Bella & Bitty: Cousins

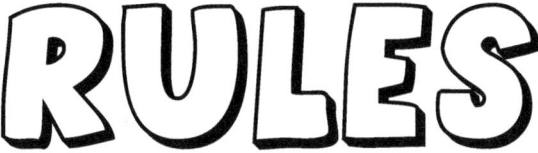

"if you obey all the rules, you miss all the fun."

katherine hepburn

Hope: Allora! Want to see my poisonous potion?!
Me: Sure! *examines old balsamic vinegar jar with leaves taped to the outside* What's in it?
Hope: It has grass in it, so it's poisonous. I made it.
Me: Oh....what do you need it for?
Hope: For danger.

Hope: But whhyy? Why can't I have anything else to eat?

Me: You snuck candy, Hope. You broke the rules. Have an apple.

Hope: I don't waaaannt an apple. Can't you fix it? Can't you just make a new rule?

Hope: Are we rich?
Me: Um...not really.
Hope: But we're not poor; we have plenty of food.
Me: We're middle-class. We're not poor, but we're not exactly rich either.
Hope: Because we have plenty of food but we don't always buy everything we want.
Me: Yep.

LATER, in my car

Hope: Wow, we sure are going fast. *pause* Allora, are you speeding?
Me: No Hopey, I'm going the speed limit.
Hope: What's the speed limit?
Me: 55.
Hope: Is that really fast?
Me: It's pretty fast, but not super fast.
Hope: Oh, *thinks* ALLORA! Are we going middle-class?! Not really fast and not really slow?
Me: ... Not really. It doesn't work that way.
Hope: *deflates* Oh.

Hope: *walks into room where her coloring pencils are, wipes nose on sleeve three times* I need a pencil sharpener.

Me: You know, it's ok to use a tissue and not your sleeve.

Hope: *stares for a moment* I can't use my sleeve as a sharpener.

Me: I know. I meant for your nose.

Hope: Well, I wasn't talking about that. *wipes nose on sleeve again*

Hope: If you were blind and stupidly driving a car it would be a stupid thing to do.

Hope: *crying, approaches Mom on porch*
Mom: Hope! What's the matter?
Hope: *silent, teary eyed*
Justin: She said a bad word.
Mom: *looks sternly at Hope* What word did you say?
Hope: *sobs, collapses in Mom's arms*
Justin: *mouths* D-A-M-N
Mom: Where did you hear such a word?!
Hope: You.
Mom: Me?! When did I say that?
Hope: Today when you yelled at Justin for picking his bug bites.
Mom: Oh. Well, sometimes grown ups say words they shouldn't because they have a lot of things on their minds. But little kids should never say them, and grown ups shouldn't too. I guess I owe you an apology, Hope.

Hope: Never interfere with the power that betrays us all.

Ashley: I'm going to spank your hinds (butt) for your insolence.
Hope: That would be awesome.
Ashley: No, it would not be awesome!
Hope: Mmmmm, debatable.

Hope: Can I have the candy on the fridge?
Anna: No.
Hope: Annnnnnaaa, please?
Anna: Hope--no!
Hope: Geez how long are you going to hold a grudge? It's been seven years--that's thirty five cat years!

Mom: Hope, you made a mess! Go clean the living room!
Hope: Clean... clean what?! I don't know what you mean.
Me: She means you need to clean up your mess.
Hope: *sighs* No one cares for poor little Hopey.

Hope: Allora, when we go to the store, can we buy a snack?

Me: I'll think about it.

Hope: Well 'think about it' is more than no, right? So thank you for saying that.

Mom: *driving to the ATM with Hope*
Hope: What are we doing?

Mom: I'm getting money. The money that Daddy earns gets stored here at the bank.

Hope: Wait, you're taking Daddy's money without even ASKING him?!

Abigail: Hope, heads or tails?
Hope: Tails.

Abigail *flips coin*: Sorry--heads. Heads or tails?

Hope: Heads.

Abigail: Mmm...tails. Heads or tails?

Hope: Tails.

Abigail: Heads. Sorry baby, heads or tails?

Hope: Heads AND tails.

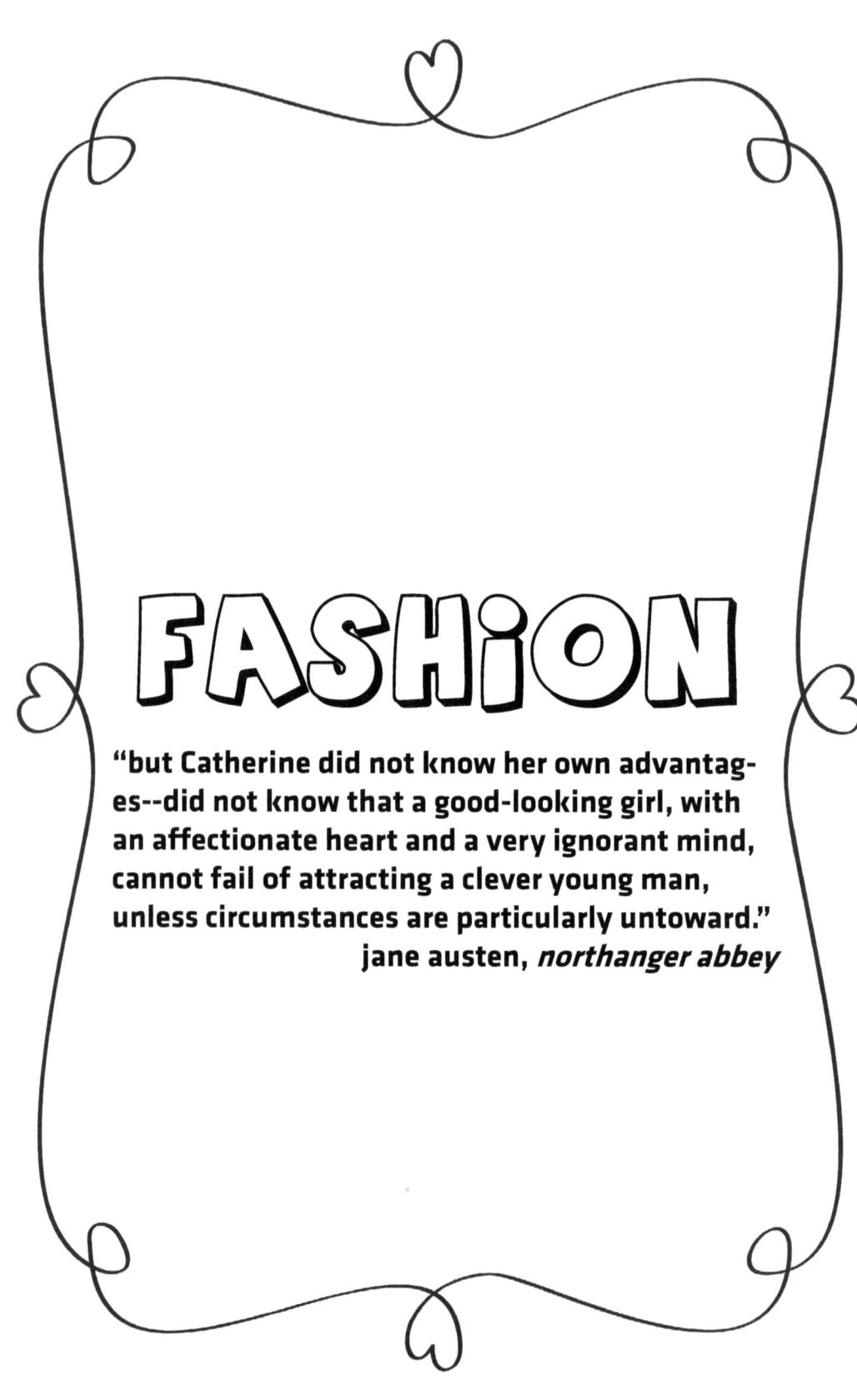

FASHION

"but Catherine did not know her own advantages--did not know that a good-looking girl, with an affectionate heart and a very ignorant mind, cannot fail of attracting a clever young man, unless circumstances are particularly untoward."

jane austen, *northanger abbey*

Hope *approaches kitchen table, holding up her hair*: Does anyone have a ponytail? *sigh, glances at Allora's pixie cut* Well I KNOW Allora doesn't have one. *walks away*

Hope: *examines one of Ashley's rings, gasps* Oh Ashley, this would make such a good fairy dog collar!

Hope: Can you paint my nails?
Me: Sure. You can only do sparkly colors or light pink.
Hope *selects sparkly purple*: Can I do it?
Me: No.
Hope: I could put a napkin down so I don't get a beating?

Hope: Don't forget to put your makeup on before bed; you'll want to look good in your dreams.

D^{ad,}

This is from me, and Allora got it on her phone to send it to you. When I did it, I wanted you. Don't that... [Don't write don't, or that.] I wanted to ask you, on this Allora's phone... Not on her phone, on the texting thing... If the nail polish in the picture, the half group, could I wear all of the nail polish--but not together. I was wondering, right now, when I sended the message. I know you love me so much so I was asking you if sometimes I could go to my friend's house. Don't be sad that I'm spending time with Allora, because I know you love me a lot. Good bye Daddy, I hope you have a nice time at work.

Love,
Hope and Allora

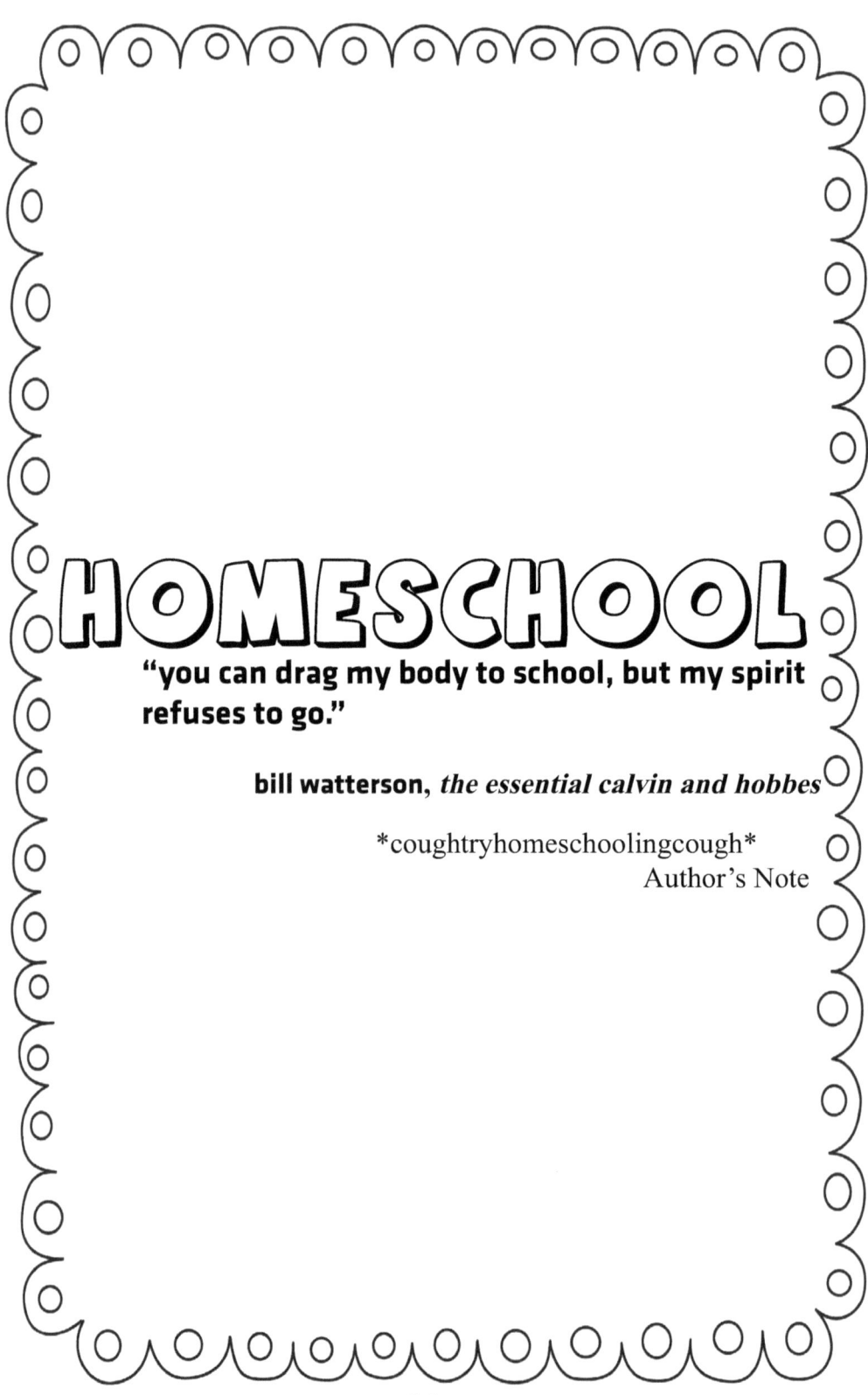

Mom: Squanto wanted to help the pilgrims. So he helped them plant the corn, and then you know what he did? He showed them how to put fish in with the corn! Do you know why he did that?

Hope: *on the edge of her chair with excitement* Cause he WANTED THE FISH TO COME UP WITH THE CORN?!?!?!?!

Mom: Um, no. It was so the fish would break down and give the corn nutrients to grow.

Hope *crestfallen*: Oh.

Hope: *eating ice cream after seeing Plymouth Rock* That's funny... I didn't think they had ice cream in those times.

Hope: Mommy, why do 'q' and 'u' always have to be together? I mean, why did they do that?

Mom: I have no idea.

Hope: Mom, who teaches kids?

Mom: Their parents usually.

Hope: But there are so many peoples in the world. How do the parents learn? How did they learn when everyone was a kid--even when all the parents were kids?

Hope: *holds up a drawing* Look what I wrote! "Hope Exit Hope Campbell."

Me: What made you want to write 'exit?'

Hope: *points to scribbles over a messed up word* Because that was a mess up.

Me: ... So exit means mistake?

Hope: No. Exit means to go or leave.

Me: So you want me to... look away from your mistake?

Hope: Yes. I want you to go away from it. Because exit means to go *runs to nearest door, smacks it, runs back* or it means to leave a mistake behind. *smacks point of paper that has messed up scribbles*

Hope: So, Allora? Are you done with school?

Me: Yes.

Hope: Forever?!

Me: Yep.

Hope: So you know everything now?

Me: Well, no.

Hope: Then you're not done with school.

✱ *Justin and Ashley attempting to explain adjectives to Hope*

Ashley: It describes a noun. Remember nouns Hope? Like a cup?

Hope: .....

Ashley: Like, look at that cup, what color is it?

Hope: White!

Ashley: Ok, so--

Hope: White! Like my skin! I'm describing myself Ashley!

POLITICS

"those who stand for nothing fall for anything."

alexander hamilton

Hope: Ashley, are you old enough to get married?

Ashley: I, um, I guess so.

Hope: How old are you?

Ashley: 19.

Hope: Whoa. You're old enough to get married!

Ashley: Too old?

Hope: No…but you have a lot of work to do.

Ashley: Why?

Hope: Well, caring for all your babies.

Ashley: Babies?! Who said I want to have babies?

Hope: Hmmm, you'd probably have to get a divorce then.

Ashley: What?! What if I just didn't want to have any right away?

Hope: Well, you're lucky then, because you're not going to get any right away.

Me: So, do you like everyone at school?

Hope: Yeah, I guess. There's one girl who's mean but I guess I still like her. And there's another girl named Carley. I like her, she's nice, but she's not very pretty. Don't tell anybody I said that...not even Mom or Dad.

Me: Oh...ok.

Hope *practicing the pledge of allegiance*: "...one nation, under God, indivisible, with liberty and ***Justins*** for all."

Hope: What's a mayor?

Anna: A mayor is someone who runs the town.

Hope:...TOWNS RUN?

Hope: Is there a king or queen of America?

Ashley: No, we have a president.

Hope: What's his name?

Ashley: President Obama

Hope: We didn't want him to win, right?

Ashley: No, not really. And he's going to be president for the next four years, until you're nine or ten.

Hope: Oh, COME ON! That's like, THREE MORE BIRTHDAYS. Well if I ever meet him, I'm certainly not going to be nice.

HOLIDAYS

"holidays are all different depending on the company and time of your life."

dominic monaghan

Hope: So, Allora, Santa doesn't use Rudolph all the time.

Me: No, I suppose he doesn't.

Hope: Sometimes he does and sometimes he doesn't. He only uses him during bad storms.

Me: Yep, that's right.

Hope: But that's not fair, he should use him all the time!

Me: Well, maybe Rudolph gets tired.

Hope: That doesn't matter. He's SPECIAL. Santa should use the special reindeer all the time.

Hope: Allora, do you know what tomorrow is?
Me: No...

Hope: St. Patrick's Day! Do you know what that means?!

Me: What does it mean?

Hope: It means we're going to have watermelon, and my friends are coming over.

Me:...Why watermelon?

Hope: Because St. Patrick brings watermelon.

Me: He does?

Hope: *smile melts off face* St. Patrick doesn't bring watermelon?

Me: Not usually.

Hope: How do we get it then?

Me: We usually buy it.

Hope: So we're not having watermelon tomorrow?

Me: Well, we could probably try to buy some. But it only grows in the summertime, so they might not even be selling it.

Hope:...

Me: Why did you think St. Patrick brought it?

Hope: *sighs* Because we have it on special days, and tomorrow is a special day, even though sometimes we might miss a special day. I think we might have missed one recently.

TECHNICALITIES

"i can't get into specifics. someday, hopefully, I'll be able to."

jason giambi

Hope: *looking for a movie which she can't find* Well, I guess it must be absent.

Mom: Justin, you should be saving your money so you could go to Minnehans with Anthony sometime.

Dad: Yeah. Then if you met some cute chick you like, you could take her for an ice cream cone.

Hope: Chickens?! Bahahahaha!!

Hope: Mom, I'm going to wrap these up [movies] and give them to the poor.

5 minutes later

Hope: Mom, actually I'm going to give them to Anna. I don't know where the poor are.

Hope: Hey Mom? You know when you give me a present to give to someone for their birthday, except that I say it's from me?

Mom: Yeah…

Hope: Well that's actually sad if you think about it. Because you're the one spending the money and then giving it to me, so it's really from you and not from me.

Mom: We told her we'd take her to the dollar store to spend her dollar. Where's your dollar, Hope?

Hope: Well, see, I don't know where I put it.

Me: You lost your first dollar?!

Hope: It wasn't my first dollar. Justin gave me one before, and I lost that one, too.

Me: Two dollars?! Do you know what you could have bought with two dollars? Candy...a pretty necklace... a spatula.

Hope: Why would I want a spatula?

Me: Or...uh...fairy glitter sparkles?

Hope: Fairy glitter sparkles? Seriously, Allora? I would just get a real fairy and get fairy dust.

Hope: Allora! I just figured out why people get sick so much.

Me: Why, Hope?

Hope: Because the world is spinning.

Me: Why does that make people sick?

Hope: Because when you spin a lot, you feel sick.

Me: *dropping Hope and Isabella off at pre-school*

Bella: All girls know that pegasuses are real. All LITTLE girls.

Hope: Big girls too. They live on the clouds.

Bella: Isn't it so funny that they have wings so they don't die?

Hope: Yeah. Ashley told me the clouds are made out of water.

Bella: Good thing they have wings.

Hope: Not really. It's hard to swim with wings in water, but they do anyway.

"don't cry because it's over; smile because it happened."

dr. seuss

Hope: Mommy I have a joke!
Mom: Ok.

Hope: How do you get off a moving camel?

Mom: I don't know. How?

Hope: I don't know, you tell me. *laughs*

Hope: Allora! I found this in the bushes, what does it say?

holds up index card with KP printed on it

Allora: "KP"

Hope: KP? What's a KP? Is it a name?

Allora: I don't know what it is, maybe it's a message.

Hope: Oh. *thinks* I thought it might be a message from Peter Pan.

Hope: Daddy wants me to find the Go Fish cards, but I can't! I tried!

Me: Hope, why do you keep losing things?

Hope: I don't know. I guess I'm just a loser.

Me: Aww, no you're not!

Hope: Not the regular kind--just the kind that loses stuff.

Hope: *looking at Rice Krispie decoration kit*: Can we make the houses now?

Amanda: We'll do it after dinner Hopey.

Hope *one hour later and the power has gone out*: Guess we shouldn't have waited till after dinner huh?

Hope: *laying on the floor crying*
Me: Hope, what's wrong?

Hope: I'm, *inhaled sob* I'm having a bad day.

Me: Why?

Hope: *groan*

Me: Well?

Hope: I can't tell.

Hope: So Dad, do you have any duck tape around here?
laughter

Dad: What do you need it for?

Hope: I need it to fix the gate.

laughter again

Hope: Guys! I can't really focus on laughing right now.

IMAGINATION

"i am enough of an artist to draw freely upon my imagination. imagination is more important than knowledge. knowledge is limited. imagination encircles the world."

albert einstein

Hope: Allora, can you close the door? I'm playing privately.

Hope: Ashley, I don't want to be a mermaid. I'm telling you so it won't come true.

Ashley: Was it a wish?

Hope: Yeah.

Hope: *inspects a flower* Nope, Thumbelina's not in here.

Hope: Did you know Anthony has an imaginary friend who eats plates?

Me: Plates? That can't taste good.

Hope: No, they cut your mouth.

Me: Does he eat anything else?

Hope: I don't know....

Me: Bowls? Does he eat cups?

Hope: Bowls?! Yeah, he probably eats bowls.

Me: So Anthony likes bowls.

Hope: Nooooo, Anthony's friend.

Me: Then who's Anthony?

Hope: Our cousin, duh.

Me: So Anthony's imaginary friend eats plates.

Hope: Yes!

Me: How did you find out?

Hope: My friend told me.

Me: Your real friend?

Hope: Yes.

Me: Which one?

Hope: She's real ok? Don't ask if she's imaginary! But her name is a secret.

Me: Can you tell me?

Hope: It's Tinkerbell.

Me: Tinkerbell?

Hope: Don't say it!! If you say it she'll cut your eyes and make a mess!!

Me: Oh... She sounds like a nice friend.

Hope: She is, she's just shy.

Hope: Allora, I really need something outside for my flower.

Me: Hope, no. It's raining.

Hope: So? It'll just take a minute.

Me: I said no!

Hope: What--you don't believe in fairies?!

Me: What does that--never mind. You have five minutes. Run.

five minutes later

Hope: I picked another flower!

Me: What did that have to do with fairies?

Hope: Nothing.

Me: You said I didn't believe in fairies?

Hope: DON'T SAY THAT! You'd better start clapping right now.

Mom: Ok kids, so what are your dreams?
Kids: .....

Mom: Well let me tell you one of mine. I'd like to write a book and get it published. Anna?

Anna: I don't necessarily want fame or fortune, because there's a lot of bad that can come with it. But I'd like my music to be known.

Ashley: Uh...I don't know. I'd like to travel I guess.

Abigail: I want to finish the story I've been writing.

Justin: I'm too young to have any dreams.

Hope: I want to be a mermaid. And a fairy.

Hope: Did you wake up last night like I told you?

Me: Why would I wake up in the night?

Hope: To see if you were still in your bed.

Me: Why wouldn't I still be in bed?

Hope: Captain Hook might have taken you.

Hope: Can I go outside?

Me: Sure.

Five minutes later

Hope: Has it been past an hour?

Me: Past an hour since what?

Hope: Well I know a movie is about an hour and mine is almost over.

Me: So… what were you waiting for?

Hope: Well, I wanted a snack.

Me: Oh, to take outside with you.

Hope: I already went outside.

Me: What do you mean you already went outside? You were gone for, like, five seconds.

Hope: It only took a minute. I had to save my fairy friend.

Me: Save her?

Hope: Yeah, her house was burning down.

Me: --

Hope: I was safe in her house because it's a fairy house. But it was burning down so I had to save her.

Me: Did you save her?

Hope: Yeah! She's right here. But she's invisible. You can't see her or hear what she's saying because only her best friends can hear her. I'm her best friend.

Me: I see.

Hope: She lives in my fort; her name is Grace. She's a winter fairy so that's why she had to stand on the ice for a second.

Me (continued): --

Hope: *sets basket on the floor* Stay there Grace! *runs outside*

Hope *after getting Eppie May to laugh continuously for five minutes*: Wow... there sure were a lot of fairies born just now.

Hope: *saying good-bye to a friend* Pretend we were forbidden from each other.

Hope: *sticks hand out car window* Pretend they're making us do that.

Bella: Ok.

Hope: So you're Obi-Wan when he had a beard.

Bella: 'k.

Hope: And I'm Anakin from the third one, so my hair was flashing in the wind. *pauses, sighs* I hate this.

Bella: *giggles* Yeah, me too.

Hope: They're going to arrest me when I get out.

Bella: Yeah.

Hope: Pretend they're doing it to the girls now: Padme and Leia. I'm Leia, you're Padme.

Bella: 'k. *mimics voice as window closes* I'm glad that's over.

Hope: Now I'm Anakin, but a different Anakin. I was Anakin from the first one. Time in!

Both silently stare out windows

Hope: *going for a walk around the farm* I'm a little scared though, foxes live out there."

Me: Foxes aren't scary. They eat bunnies, not people.

Hope: They eat bunnies? BUNNIES? THEY ATE MY BUNNIES?!

Me: Er- no. Your bunnies ran away to get married and have babies.

Hope: *sniffs* Bunnies can't get married.

Me: *eagerly* Sure they do!

Hope: How?

Me: They say I love you and that's it and they're happy together.

Hope: *silence*: The foxes probably eat the babies then.

Me: *facepalm*

Hope: Allora! Look what I found!
Me: oh, it's a helicopter seed.

Hope: Helicopter? It's a funny helicopter, the only way it goes is down.

Me: That is funny.

Hope: *chuckling to herself* Strange little helicopter that doesn't go anywhere and flies without people and dying. So funny!

Hope: I want to tell you a bad secret.
Me: Are you going to get in trouble if you tell me?

Hope: No, it's just a bad secret and bad news.

Me: ok...

Hope: So I was putting a hurt bee into my fairy cradle. And it pinched me, and I started bleeding and screaming.

Me: So why is that a secret?

Hope: I hurt myself, so it's a bad thing. And I didn't want to tell anyone, so it's a secret.

Hope: Cats are like vampires to fish.
Anna: How'd you figure?
Hope: Because cats eat fish.

Hope: There's lots of water making floods, isn't there, Allora?
Me: Well, there are a lot of puddles.
Hope: The world is having a shower.

Mom: Sure has been raining a lot.
Hope: The clouds must be tired.

Hope: Allora, what do wild horses do if they have nobody to ride them?

Me: They run around and eat, mostly.

Hope: That's what their priorities are if they're wild?

Me: Yep

Abby *examining our cat's ear, which has been bitten*: Well, he's sort of a stupid kitty. He keeps getting into fights.

Hope: ABIGAIL! I'm going to tell God what you said!

Abby: ....why?

Hope: Because God gave us this beautiful creature and you are not even thankful for him! So I'm going to tell God!

Hope *Sitting with Ashley on the porch. Ashley puts a flower barrette in her hair to make Hope laugh*

Ashley: Don't I look pretty, Hope? There's flowers growing out of my head!

Hope: Wow, you must be really dirty.

Ashley: *smile fades* Wha-what do you mean?"

Hope: Plants grow where there's dirt, Ashley.

Ashley: Oh…

Hope: *picking grass* Allora, I'm making bird nests.

Me: Oh really?

Hope: Yeah! I pick the grass and put it in this tree.

Me: You're doing a good job.

Hope: Yeah. The birds are going to be like, 'this nest is too nice, it must be somebody else's home.' But I'm going to make them anyway.

Hope *telling Mom a story*: And the mermaid is sad.

Mom: Why is the mermaid sad?

Hope: Because she lost her mermaid suit.

Me: Wait... what's a mermaid suit? I thought mermaids had fishtails?

Hope: No, they wear mermaid suits.

Mom: So it's a regular girl in a mermaid suit? What happens if they take it off?

Hope: Well, I guess you'll have to wait until you see a mermaid.

Hope: *moaning about the heat* Why is the sun so close to the earth today?

Hope: *attempting to kill lots of bees with bee spray*

Ashley: Hope! You don't have to kill all of them! What will the other bees think?

Hope: Ashley, the other bees don't care. They just get more honey.

Hope: *eating a hotdog, groans, puts head on table*

Anna: What's wrong?

Hope: I wish I was a pig.

Anna: ....

Hope: Then I would have room to keep eating this.

Me: Do you remember when we went on vacation and there were wild horses?

Hope: Yeah! I remember when we touch them they disappeared.

Me: Um…

Hope: Cause they were magical.

Me: They weren't—the ones on the beach?

Hope: I know that!

Me: They were just wild; they weren't magic.

Hope: No, they were. Daddy told me. If you touch them they would go away.

Me: Oh…

Hope: They would disappear.

Me: *coughs* That's probably true. I never touched them so I, uh, didn't know.

Hope: What does life mean?
Mom: What does it mean to you?

Hope: Well, it means two things. First it means that you're alive. And second, Bella says 'life' if she doesn't want to play anything.

WORK

"nothing will work unless you do."
maya angelou

Mom: Hope, go tell Justin to make Dad and I coffee.

Hope: *huffing and puffing and not wanting to do assigned task*

Mom: Hope, I do everything for you! I wash your clothes, clean your room, teach you school, make you food, arrange your playdates—everything! I'm your Cinderella!

Hope: *silent*

Mom: That's right. Everything. I even buy you toys and—

Hope: *interrupts* Cinderella SCRUBS FLOORS!

Mom: *laughs till she cries* No, I just scrub TOILETS!

Hope: So... Are you going to work?

Me *in waitressing uniform*: Yes.

Hope: But what do you do at work? Do you make the food?

Me: No, I bring it to people.

Hope: Oh, so you're a servant.

Me: Yep. That's exactly what I am.

Me: Hope, hop off your pony, it's time for you to clean him up as a thank you.

Hope: Ok, where's the stuff?

Me: You know where it is.

Hope: Over here?

Me: Yep. And you have to make him look really nice. When you think you're done, come get me and I'll check.

Hope: *walks past grinning with a box of brushes* I'm done!

Me: Very funny.

Hope: Can you get paper for me from the parlor?

Ashley: No! I'd have to walk all the way over to the computer and back.

Hope: I do things for you all the time!

Ashley: What do you do for me?

Hope: Uh…

Ashley: Do you give me baths?

Hope: No.

Ashley: Do you help me get dressed?

Hope: No.

Ashley: Do you do my hair?

Hope: No.

Ashley: Well?

Hope: I carry books for you sometimes when you go to bed.

Ashley: You carry books for me to read to you in bed.

Hope: Well sometimes I help you clean my room!

FAITH

"do not think that love, in order to be genuine, has to be extraordinary. what we need is to love without getting tired. be faithful in small things because it is in them that your strength lies."

mother teresa

Hope and Ashley gathering flowers for the Mary Statue
Ashley: Hope, aren't these pretty for Mary?
Hope: Yeah, but she won't like them.
Ashley: Why?
Hope: Cause Mommy said she only likes prayers.

Hope: Bella, "Amen" means "I believe" in Aladdin.
Ashley: ... Hope, do you mean "in Latin?"
Hope: Yeah! In Latin!

Mom: Hope, look at the sky. It looks like a gateway to heaven.

Hope: Oh yes it does. Looks like Jesus is up there.

Mom: Yes, he is always looking out for us. No more pain or sadness.

Hope: No more boo-boos either because the ground is nice and soft!

Hope: Mom, come see this—Hurry!

Mom *examining Hope's glow in the dark rosary*: Wow Hope, I can see it from here.

Hope: It's glowing cause you're holy.

Hope: What is that?

Me: A devilled egg.

Hope: Is it bad?

Me: No...?

Hope: But the Devil is bad.

Reading Genesis, about God hanging stars in the sky

Hope: Wait, he hung the stars in the sky?

Mom: Yes.

Hope: He hung them…like *decorations*?

Mom *reading Hope stories from the Bible*: ..for they shall be the sons of god.

Hope: Or the daughters.

Hope: What does 'Amen' mean?
Abigail: 'I believe.'

Hope *laughs*: Amen in fairies!

Reading a story that featured a not-pretty princess

Hope: *sigh* I so wish that she was a beautiful princess.

Ashley: Hope, she doesn't have to be beautiful for the prince to love her.

Hope: She doesn't?

Ashley: No! He might love her for her personality.

Hope: What's a personality?

Ashley: It's what makes you, you.

Hope: Well God makes you, so a personality is God.

Hope: Can you take me ice skating tonight?

Me: No, maybe next weekend.

Hope: NEXT WEEKEND?!

Me: Sorry Hopey, we need to go to church tonight.

Hope: Are you kidding?

Me: No.

Hope: When we go to church we come back at lunch time.

Me: Tonight is special; we're going to confession.

Hope: What's confession?

Me: You go to church and tell the priest your sins.

Hope: *silent, mouth open*

Me: You tell him all the things you've done bad.

Hope: *slumps* Awwwwww....

Me: Don't worry about it, you're too little.

Hope: *instant relief* Thank goodness.

Me: *Still driving Hope and Bella to pre-school*

Hope: Have you ever seen Black Beauty? I have. Or I saw one that's based off the real one.

Bella: I've seen the real one, it's so good.

Hope: Yeah, except in the real one, the horse dies.

silence

Hope: But that's not too sad because we're going to die soon anyway.

Bella: No we're not! We have to be grown ups first.

Hope: It only feels like a little bit of time to God.

Bella: I know. God never dies.

Hope: I know. God is the biggest one.

Tooth Fairy:

IM SRRE THET I HAF LOST MI TOOTH. BUT THIS CRD IS A GIFT. MI PARINS TOLD ME TO PUT MI TOOTH IN MI PILO. BUT I DID NOT LISIN. PLES GIF ME MUN E.

IM INFUYTING YOU TO MI HWS TOMRRO FOR A TE PRDE.

-Translation-

Tooth Fairy:

I'm sorry that I have lost my tooth. But this card is a gift. My parents told me told me to put my tooth in my pillow. But I did not listen.

Please give me money.

I'm inviting you to my house tomorrow for a tea party.

"i don't know half of you half as well as I should like, and i like less than half of you half as well as you deserve."

bilbo baggins, *the fellowship of the ring*

Hope: *whispering to Bella in the back seat*
Mom: Hope, what are you saying?"

Hope: Nothing.

Mom: Please tell me, Hope! Don't keep secrets from your mother—I'll cry!

Hope: Don't worry Mom, I have other secrets.

Hope: Allora!

Me: Yes baby?

Hope: Are you putting your jammies on?

Me: Yes baby.

Hope: Then I will. are you going to bed now?

Me: No baby.

Hope: Then I won't.

pause

Hope: Allora? Do you change your panties at night?

Me: Yes baby.

Hope: Then I will.

Mom: *talking to Hope about Eppie* How could you be jealous of that little baby? Isn't she the cutest thing in the world?

Hope: I think she's cute.

Hope: Mommy, do you remember the stick race I won?

Mom: Yes.

Hope: Well I don't think I really won.

Mom: Why would you say that?

Hope: Well, I saw another human before me.

Mom: *laughing* Well, it doesn't matter because mommies clap even if you don't win.

Abigail: *looking at a letter Hope is writing to a friend* "I am wanted..." What does that mean?

Hope: It means I have a family and they love me.

*almost everyone

Hope: Ashley! So summer came before winter right?

Ashley: Yes Hopey, that's right.

Hope: I'm not at all familiar with it. Like when mommy used to hang up the laundry and I was playing. But there was one time I looked over and she was gone.

Mom: Hope, no! You're breaking my heart! How do you know that I just didn't go inside for more laundry or clothes pins?

Hope: No, you were gone for too long I waited. *pauses* Not gone from the house, just gone from outside.

Anna: Hope, I love you most in the whole wide world.

Hope: ANNA! No you don't.

Anna: ?

Hope: You love God, Jesus, then Mary, then the Saints. Right?

Anna: Well I--

Hope: Right Anna? I'm last. You've known me for the least amount of time anyway, so you must love me less.

Anna: Hope! I love you most!

Hope: Anna, enough.

Justin: Am I in your book?

Me *grumpily*: No. It's a book of Hope quotes. You don't say Hope quotes. Hope says Hope quotes.

Justin: Can I try?

Me: All you two ever do is fight.

Justin *tries to start conversation*: Hope, why don't you want to be a fairy anymore?

Hope: *stares sullenly, pouts, doesn't answer*

Anna: Mom, you need to order this movie, it's called 'A New Hope.'

Me: Not Star Wars.

Hope: A new HOPE?

Mom: What's it about?

Hope: If you wanted a new Hope, you'd have to put me back in Mommy's belly.

Hope: Allora, what does 'Bitty' mean?
Me: It's Angelina's nickname.

Hope: So what does it mean?

Me: It means 'Angelina.'

Hope: No! You know how names mean something and Angelina's name means something?

Me: Yes, but nicknames just mean the person they're for. You know how we call you Del Ronso?

Hope: Yeah.

Me: What does that mean?

Hope: *points to self*

Me: It's the same for Bitty. Bitty means Angelina.

Hope: *stares, puts forehead in hand* You're just not explaining it so that it makes sense.

ACCOMPLISHMENTS

"to be yourself in a world that is constantly trying to make you something else is the greatest accomplishment."

ralph waldo emerson

Hope: Allora! Do you want to see me ride without cartwheels?

Me: Wait, what?

Hope: Do you want to see me ride without cartwheels?

Me: Do you mean that you're doing cartwheels or riding your bike?

Hope: I'm riding my bike without the side wheels.

Me: They're called training wheels.

Hope: Oh.

Me: But you can call them training wheels, too.

Hope: Ok, so do you want to see me ride without them?

Me: Absolutely.

Mom: I'm having a hard time with you turning six. Can we just write that you're staying five and just pretend?

Hope: No, Mom, you'll get over it.

Mom: How?

Hope: Once it passes.

Mom *laughs*: But how do you know?

Hope: Well, cause when I turned five you cried and then you got over it.

Hope: Yeah, I swam in the deep end.

Me: Did you go under the water?

Hope: Yep.

Me: Did you open your eyes?

Hope: Well…

Me: You would have, right, if you had goggles?

Hope: I can do it under the water with goggles or without goggles.

Me: Wow. It's pretty cool right?

Hope: Yeah, but sometimes you get stuff in your eyes.

Me: Yeah, like Chlorine?

Hope: Like Poop!

Me: Probably just Chlorine.

Hope: And dirt!

Me: *sigh*

Hope: And rocks!

Hope: Did Mary and Joseph like each other?

Mom: Of course Hope, they were married.

Hope: That's because God made them get married.

Ashley: *picks up up a set of keys tied together* Hope... what is this?

Hope: The keys to my heart.

Mom: Allora, you should go to Justin's military ball. We're all going; it'll be fun.

Hope: A BALL?!

Me: Mmm, I think I'll pass.

Hope: Allora! You have to go! If you do, someone will fall in love with you!

Hope: I hope you have a good time, and I hope you have a good day.

Hope: Mommy, were you disgusted when you started kissing Daddy on the lips?

Mom: Why would you ask such a question?

Hope: Because it's disgusting!

FiLM

"everything I learned I learned from the movies."

audrey hepburn

H ope: Allora, do you want to have a light saber battle?

Hope *facing Angelina with one hand outstretched during a Star Wars Play*: We're force-choking each other! *Each's hand starts to tremble, and they pass out*

Hope: * watching Star Wars Episode 3 right before Obi-Wan chops off Anakin's arm.*

Anna: *walks into room singing*

Hope: ANNA! STOOPPPPP!! This is the best part!!

Hope *holding something behind her back*: I got a lightsaber. *giggles* Just kidding. It's just an ice pop.

Watching the Ten Commandments' chariot scene

Hope: The Egyptians are brats. GET OUT! Whoa! I'm getting mad now baby!!

Me: We watched Mirror, Mirror, with Julia Roberts.

Mom: I don't think I've seen that one.

Hope: It has bad words in it.

Mom: Don't you say them!

Hope: It had "shut" AND "up" together in it.

Mom: *gasp!*

Hope: Mommy, I'm bad.

Mom: Why are you bad?

Hope: Because red is bad in Star Wars and red is my favorite color.

Talking with Mom about whether Hope can see Mirror Mirror

Hope: What we're you talking about?

Me: Nothing... we weren't talking about anything.

Hope: Yes you were, you were talking about taking me to the movies.

Me: Well, we did sort of talk about that. We don't know if the movie is too scary for you or not. So I'm going to see it first, and then Mom will take you to see it later.

Hope: How about you take me with you and tell me when to close my eyes.

Me: It still might be too scary for you, I don't know yet.

Hope: Well how about you call the Movie Man and ask him if it's scary and, if he says no, than I can come with you!

Ashley: Do you even know what Ursela wants?

Hope: Yeah, she wants supreme power over the ocean.

Ashley: No.

Hope: she wants Ariel?

Ashley: No.

Hope: Prince Eric?

Ashley: No.

Hope: She wants King Trident's….trident?

Amanda: Huh, I never realized how weird that sounded before.

Me *listening to music*: This is from Pocahontas.

Hope: Mmmmm, I didn't like that one. The girl shouldn't be taking care of the guy.

Me: Why not?

Hope: It's a more romantic love story if the guy has to save the girl from the villain. Much better.

Hope: In Narnia, why does Santa come in spring?

Hope *talking about favorite Star Wars Parts*: Bella, *mimics groaning* Ben... Ben... Dagoba system. *giggles* Do you remember that?

Bella: No...

Hope: I do. Remember when he's trapped in the snow, Bella?

Me: When they put him in the guts?

Hope: Yeah! When they put him in the guts!

Bella: Eww...

Hope: *delighted* I know!

Hope: *watching Star Wars for the first time*
Darth Vader: "Luke, I am your father."
Hope: Wow. He sure is a bad father.

Me: What's your favorite game now?

Hope & Bella: Star Wars.

Me: Who plays who?

Hope: Sometimes Angelina is Anakin, sometimes I'm Anakin, sometimes Angelina is Luke—well, Allora.

Me: What about you, Bella?

Hope: Why do we always have to explain it, Allora?

Me: Because I wanna know! Bella, who do you play?

Bella: Sometimes I'm Padme in the second one or sometimes I'm Leia from the fourth one.

Hope: Sometimes she's Anakin or Luke.

Bella: Or sometimes I'm Anakin from the first one.

Hope: Sometimes she's Anakin from the second one or the third one.

Me: mmm, how come you don't like explaining that to me? I think that's cool!

Hope: *exasperated* Because what if we change characters or we forget?

Me: That's ok! Forgetting is ok!

Hope: Why do we always have to tell you what we always play?

Me: Because I like to know what you're up to!

Hope: Well, what if we can't explain it because it's too hard.

Me: Well, you're doing a good job now. *pauses* You're doing a great job.

Hope: *silent*

Me: Yeah? YEAH?

Hope: Yeah!

ACKNOWLEDGMENTS

Allora: This book wouldn't have happened without the help of my family. Both through their inspiring Hope's quotes, but also for all their help collecting the quotes through the long year I decided to keep track of them. Thank you!

This book also wouldn't have happened without the financial support of both friends and family who were interested enough to buy a copy. Thank you for supporting us!

Hope: Well I don't have anyone to thank because no one helped me think of funny things to say.

But I do want to thank Anna, Ashley, Abigail, Mommy and Daddy, Angelina, Bella, Justin, Grandma and Bobba, Emily, Genny, Allora, Amanda, Vanessa, Kristen, Aunt Leslie and Uncle Timmy, the Priest, and Uncle Steve. And I love my whole family, too. Thanks for them!

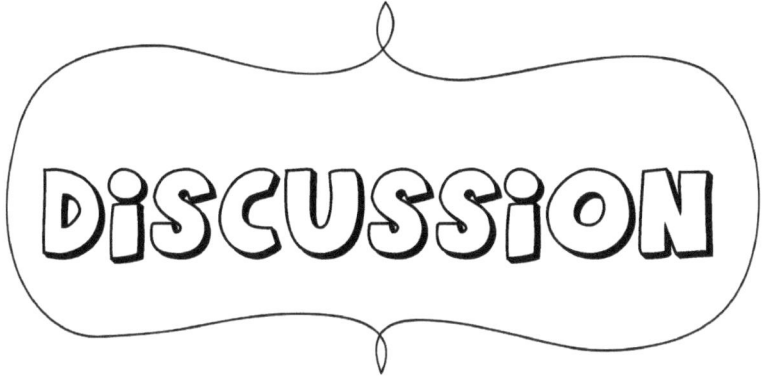

I've always thought that, beneath the charm and amusement, there's something powerful about each and every Hope Quote. Did something interesting strike you about a particular quote? Do you have a favorite or a wish you could comment on one? Or do you have your own collection of "Hope Quotes" from the kids in your life? Visit our blog or follow us on Facebook to share!

Post your thoughts, comments, or questions on *A Hopeful World's* Blog:

        ahopefulworld.blogspot.com

Hope Campbell: Hope is six years old and is in First Grade. She loves to go to her friends' houses, her birthday parties, watching movies, going in the hayloft, riding Connor, playing *Star Wars*, Pilgrims, and Fairies. Her favorite movies are *Star Wars* and *Jumangi*. Her favorite book is *Aquamarine*. She would like to be an artist, guitar player, doctor, and shoveling archeologist when she grows up. She lives in Western New York with her family, pony (Connor), dog (Lucy), and cat (Oliver).

Allora Campbell: Allora is a twenty-three year old recent college graduate who is sorting out adulthood. When she isn't writing, managing her family's retirement farm for handicapped horses, or restoring their 19th century home, she enjoys reading and doing graphic design. She's previously published a short story, "Stalled," in the *Summerset Review*. Allora currently works as an Adjunct Professor, a Social Media Specialist, and as a MSR for a Credit Union. She resides with her family in Western New York.

This is Allora and Hope's first book.

THE END

"hope has two beautiful daughters; their names are anger and courage. anger at the way things are, and courage to see that they do not remain as they are."

-augstine of hippo

www.ingramcontent.com/pod-product-compliance
Lightning Source LLC
Chambersburg PA
CBHW042326150426
43193CB00001B/3